INT

To
my mother-in-law
Helene Riehle
and
in memory of
my father-in-law
William Charles Riehle (1905–1979)
who invariably danced The Dying Swan *after vodka*

RONALD HARWOOD

INTERPRETERS
A fantasia on English and Russian themes

AMBER LANE PRESS

All rights whatsoever in this play are strictly reserved and
application for performance etc. should be made before
rehearsal to:
Judy Daish Associates Ltd.
83 Eastbourne Mews
London W2 6LQ

No performance may be given unless a licence has been
obtained.

First published in 1986 by
Amber Lane Press Ltd.
9 Middle Way
Oxford OX2 7LH

Typset in Baskerville by
Oxford Computer Typesetting Ltd.

Printed in Great Britain by
Cotswold Press Ltd., Oxford

ISBN: 0 906399 67 X

CHARACTERS

GORKIN
VIKTOR BELAEV
RICHARD POINTER
NADIA OGILVIE-SMITH
ZHIGALIN
SOPHIA, LADY OGILVIE-SMITH

The play takes place in the Foreign and Commonwealth Office, and in a flat in Ennismore Gardens,
London.

Interpreters was first presented by Robert Fox Ltd. and Duncan C. Weldon in association with Michael Medwin for Memorial Films at The Queen's Theatre, London, on 19th November, 1985. It was directed by Peter Yates, with the following cast:

NADIA:	Maggie Smith
GORKIN:	Jeffry Wickham
POINTER:	John Moffatt
VIKTOR:	Edward Fox
ZHIGALIN:	Dan Meaden
SOPHIA:	Doreen Mantle

Designed by Farrah
Lighting by Rory Dempster

A note to encourage the actor playing Viktor Belaev

After the first reading of *Interpreters*, Edward Fox, who was to create Viktor Belaev, announced that he would have to learn some Russian if the part and the play were to be effective. He treated the fact that he knew not a single word of the language as an irritating but minor detail. Undaunted, or apparently undaunted, he set about the task. It is entirely accurate to record that the only person who showed any signs of being at all daunted was the author: I felt I had laid on my leading man an impossible burden.

While writing the play, I had thought that only the actor playing Gorkin would have to speak Russian. (This was fairly obvious, I suppose, since the character doesn't have a word of English in the piece.) But I had somehow persuaded myself, naively I now realise, that the actor cast as Viktor would, when Russian was expected of him, get away with mumbling, or with having his back to the audience, or even with gobbledegook. I could not have been more wrong. Fox pointed out that to make Viktor a believable bilingual Soviet interpreter it was essential that the first words he uttered should be in Russian. This turned out to be crucially important from the point of view of both actor and audience. Once it had been established in the audience's mind that the actor was speaking Russian, it meant that as the play progressed the actor needed only to say one or two key words in the foreign language to continue the sleight-of-tongue.

This method worked especially well in the two Foreign Office scenes; it was, however, to prove inadequate when it came to Viktor's confession after the party in Act Two. In this scene, Nadia is obliged to interpret (or misinterpret) her lover's version of events as he presents them to his superior. Maggie Smith, whose theatrical instincts are the finest I have encountered, rightly forecast that it would be impossible for her either to impart the emotional impact of what he was saying or to time her translations and interjections if she (and the audience) did not hear him speak in Russian. To this Edward Fox wholeheartedly agreed.

With the essential and sympathetic assistance of Dmitri Makaroff, the production's Russian Vocal Coach, Fox began to learn Viktor's Russian which had been written out for him in transliterated form and which is now part of the text. He worked from the transliterations and from cassette recordings made by Makaroff. He had also to rehearse the play. After four weeks (the entire rehearsal period) he had mastered the sounds. It seemed to the rest of us an astonishing achievement.

Fox himself claims that he did not find it all that difficult; he even suggests that the process was enjoyable. The fact is that, over an average rehearsal period, he managed to learn, parrot-fashion, chunks of foreign dialogue which were totally convincing and which fooled many a native Russian speaker including, I am told, more than one visiting Soviet diplomat.

Ronald Harwood

ACT ONE

Light on NADIA, *seated.*

She is in her forties, dressed sombrely, a touch severe, spinsterish. She wears dark glasses. Her left hand trembles a little.

NADIA: It's a question of interpretation. That's predictable coming from me, since I am, or was, an interpreter. This inquiry, presumably, will determine the correct tense. [*She tries to smile.*] Forgive these dark glasses. I have not been well. I'm not sure how to describe my state, but the word that springs instantly to mind is crying. I've been crying. Yes, that seems a perfectly adequate description. I've been crying more or less continuously, ever since — how long is it — only forty-eight hours? But my tears, I know, are trivial, at least from your point of view, from the point of view of security, and so on and so forth. Although Mr. Pointer said recently that nothing in our work was trivial. Mr. Pointer will, no doubt, in due course, be giving his own interpretation of what happened. For the present, all I want to say is that I had no intention of endangering my country. The worst, I believe, that should be said of me is I acted foolishly or selfishly, whichever is applicable. The truth is I endangered no one but myself.

[*Pause.*]

May I say something about myself before interpreting the events as I experienced them? It may help to explain my actions, although I have recently come to the conclusion that there is an irrational element in my behaviour which defies explanation. I want to correct an impression that you may have of me, that I know is current. I am well aware that I am regarded as the Old Maid of Whitehall. I once overheard the Secretary of State — he was at school with my father, you know — I once overheard him, saying to one of those bright young men we seem to have about the place nowadays, he said, 'The trouble with Nadia is that she's not getting it regular.' To which the bright young man replied, 'If she's getting it at all.' To which the Secretary of State rejoined, 'If she's ever got it.' I repeat these remarks not because they hurt me particularly but because I think I ought to warn you against judging by appearances. Mine or anyone else's.

[*Pause.*]

Lights grow. NADIA *removes her glasses and walks into —*
A small conference room in the Foreign and Commonwealth Office, London. Summer. Mid-afternoon.

On one side of a conference table sits GORKIN, *late forties, an apparently genial man. Beside him sits his interpreter,* VIKTOR BELAEV, *about the same age, attractive and elegant. He speaks English without the trace of an accent. Behind them, solitary and apart, sits* ZHIGALIN, *nondescript, mid-fifties. He does not partake in the discussion. On the other side sits* RICHARD POINTER, *the Deputy Head of the Soviet Department, late forties, a dash of North Country in his voice.* NADIA *sits beside him.*

For the most part VIKTOR *translates English into Russian for* GORKIN'S *benefit.* NADIA *translates Russian into English for* POINTER'S.

GORKIN: Blagodaryu vas, gospodin Pointer, za tyoplyye slova privyetstviya.

NADIA: Thank you for those warm words of welcome, Mr. Pointer.

GORKIN: Srazu skazhu, my ochen' rady byt' zdyes' v Londonye v vashem Forin-Ofisye s yevo bogatym istoricheskim naslyediyem.

NADIA: Let me say at once, how pleased we are to be here in London in the Foreign and Commonwealth Office, with all its historic associations.

GORKIN: My privyezli vam privyet iz Moskvy...

NADIA: We bring you greetings from Moscow...

GORKIN: ...i s nyetyerpyeniyem ozhidayem obsuzhdyeniya programmy myeropriyatii v svyazi s pryedstoyashchim ofitsial'nym vizitom v Angliyu Pryedsyedatyelya Pryezidiuma Vyerkhovnovo Sovyeta SSSR Nikolaya Lyeonidovicha Styepanova.

NADIA: We look forward to discussing the social arrangements for the forthcoming state visit of His Excellency, the President of the Soviet Union, Nikolai Stepanov.

GORKIN: Pryezidyent lichno podcherknul...

NADIA: I have been instructed by the President himself...

GORKIN: ...i ya tozhe tak dumayu...

NADIA: ...and it is also my personał wish...

GORKIN: ...chto pyeryegovory s Vyelikobritanniyei dolzhny prokhodit' v dukhye dyelovitoi zaintyeryesovannosti i vzaimoponimaniya.

NADIA: ...to be entirely co-operative.

[*When* POINTER *speaks,* VIKTOR *translates into* GORKIN'S *ear.*]

POINTER: Thank you very much, Mr. Gorkin.

VIKTOR: Blagodaryu vas, Mister Gorkin.

POINTER: Right. Well. Now, then. Let's see.

VIKTOR: Khorosho...

POINTER: There are just the three main topics we should discuss.

VIKTOR: Nam nado obsudit' tri glavnykh problyemy.

POINTER: The President's arrival and departure...

VIKTOR: Pribytiye i otyezd pryezidyenta...

POINTER: ...the Prime Minister's dinner...

VIKTOR: ...uzhin u Prem'yer-Ministra...

POINTER: ...and the visit to the theatre.

VIKTOR: ...i posyeshcheniye tyeatra.

POINTER: I don't foresee any difficulties. Routine, really.

VIKTOR: Ya nye pryedvizhu nikakikh oslozhnyenii. Obychnaya rutina.

POINTER: [*to* VIKTOR] Am I going too fast for you, Mr. Belaev?

VIKTOR: Not at all. Thank you. Your pace is my pace.

POINTER: Good. [*to* GORKIN] If you are agreeable, I should like to begin with the PM's dinner.

VIKTOR: Yesli soglasny, ya by nachal s bankyeta.

POINTER: I think, perhaps, we ought first to consider the menu. Don't you?

VIKTOR: Snachala po-moyemu nado ogovorit' myenyu.

GORKIN: Eto myenya ustrayivayet.

NADIA: [*translating*] I would like that.

POINTER: We thought we'd begin with those little bits...

VIKTOR: Po-nashemu luchshye nachat' s etikh malyen'kikh shtuchek...

POINTER: ...those snacks so beloved of Russians — [*He searches for the word.*] — what d'you call them?

VIKTOR: Zakuski.

NADIA: Zakuski.

POINTER: Zakuski, exactly. You know the sort of thing, Mr. Gorkin. A pickled herring, a gorkin, a gherkin... [*He tries to smile at his mistake.*] Russian salad...

VIKTOR: ...vinyegryet...

POINTER: ...a radish, with, of course, vodka.

VIKTOR: Nu, i konyechno, vodka.

[*Deadly silence. Then,* GORKIN *explodes.*]

GORKIN: Nyet.

[*Stunned silence.*]

NADIA: No.

GORKIN: Nyet, nyet, nyet.

NADIA: [*translating*] No, no.

POINTER: [*totally bewildered*] What seems to be the problem?

VIKTOR: V chyom zhe problyema?

GORKIN: Vodka, nyet.

NADIA: Vodka, no.

POINTER: But we want to make Mr. Stepanov feel as much at home as possible.

VIKTOR: ...kak doma.

POINTER: Doesn't he like vodka?

VIKTOR: Razvye on nye lyubit vodki?

GORKIN: Da, konyechno on lyubit vodku.

NADIA: Yes, the President likes vodka all right.

POINTER: Well then?

VIKTOR: Nu?

GORKIN: No pryezidyent nye zhelayet, chtoby na obyedye,

ustroyennom v yevo chest' vashim Prem'yer-Minis-trom, podavali vodku.

NADIA: The President does not wish to drink vodka at a dinner hosted by your Prime Minister.

POINTER: The President likes vodka...

VIKTOR: Lyubit'-to lyubit.

POINTER: ...but he won't drink it at the PM's dinner.

VIKTOR: ...nye stanyet u Prem'yer-Ministra.

GORKIN: Imyenno.

NADIA: Exactly.

POINTER: Why ever not?

VIKTOR: Pochemu-zhe nyet?

GORKIN: Viditye li, gospodin Pointer...

NADIA: Frankly, Mr. Pointer...

GORKIN: ...u nas v Soyuzye vodka — v osnovnom — dlya nuzhd prolyetariata.

NADIA: ...in the Soviet Union, vodka is considered a work-ing-class drink.

POINTER: Working-class?

VIKTOR: Rabochi klass...

GORKIN: Vodka, odno iz samykh vydayushchikhsya dostizhe-nii Sovyetskovo Soyuza. Ona dostupna vsyem.

NADIA: It is one of the many outstanding achievements of the Soviet Union. Vodka is available to all.

POINTER: So I believe.

GORKIN: Odnako, kogda pryezidyent za granitsei...

NADIA: But when the President travels abroad...

GORKIN: ...on dolzhen byt' prinyat so vsyemi pochestyami i uvazheniyem podobayushchimi lidyeru byelikovo naroda.

NADIA: ...he must be treated with all the honour and respect due to the leader of a great people.

GORKIN: Yesli by vasha korolyeva posyetila Moskvu...

NADIA: If the Queen were to come to Moscow...

GORKIN: ...my by nye stali ugoshchat' yeyo tyoplym pivom.

NADIA: ...you wouldn't expect us to serve her warm beer.

POINTER: What do you suggest we give him, then?

VIKTOR: ...yemu podavat'?

GORKIN: Shato Latur.

NADIA: Château Latour.
POINTER: Château Latour.
GORKIN: Pyat'dyesyat-tryetyevo goda. Pryekrasnyi god.
NADIA: 1953. A great year.
GORKIN: Ili mozhno Shato Margo sorok-syed'movo goda.
NADIA: Or Château Margaux 1947.
GORKIN: Ryech' vyed' idyot o samom Pryezidyentye Sovyets-
    kovo Soyuza.
NADIA: We are talking about the President of the Soviet
    Union.
GORKIN: A chto kasayetsya vodki, to dazhe nye govoritye.
NADIA: Vodka? Forget it.
GORKIN: Davaitye soglasimsya na bordo…
NADIA: We will have Bordeaux…
GORKIN: …prem'yer kryu…
NADIA: …*premier cru*…
GORKIN: …apyelyasion controlye…
NADIA: …*appellation contrôlée*…
GORKIN: …mis an butei o shato…
NADIA: …*mis en bouteille au château*…
GORKIN: Nu, yesli uzh vam tak nuzhny yeshcho pryedlozhe-
    niya, togda, nu, naprimyer…
NADIA: And if you want some other suggestions, I'll give
    them to you.
GORKIN: …khorosheye burgundskoye vino bylo by nye-
    vryedno.
NADIA: A good burgundy wouldn't come amiss.
GORKIN: Kot de Nu-i nyeplokho…
NADIA: Côte de Nuits, for example.
GORKIN: …ili, skazhem, Shamberten shest'dyesyat-shestovo
    goda…
NADIA: …a Chambertin 1966…
GORKIN: …tak-zhe budyet vpolyne priyemlyemo.
NADIA: …perfectly acceptable.
GORKIN: A pro vodku, bol'she nye slova.
NADIA: But please, let us not mention vodka again.
            [*Awkward pause.*]
POINTER: I'm afraid I'm not in a position to negotiate this.
VIKTOR: …nye v sostoyanii.

GORKIN: Da chto vy mnye mozgi v kruchivayetye?

NADIA: What are you telling me?

GORKIN: Zamyestityel' nachal'nika sovyetskovo otdyela v britanskom Forin-Ofisye nye vlastyen otmyenit' zakaz na vodku i zamyenit' yeyo prilichnym vinom?

NADIA: That you, Deputy Head of the Soviet Department in the British Foreign and Commonwealth Office, cannot cancel vodka and order a decent wine?

GORKIN: Ni v zhist' nye povyeryu.

NADIA: I don't believe this.

POINTER: I am not in the habit of lying, Mr. Gorkin. What I say is the truth.

VIKTOR: ...ya govoryu pravdu.

POINTER: I don't have the authority to negotiate on this point.

VIKTOR: ...dal'she pyeryegovory.

GORKIN: Odnu minutku, pozhaluista.

NADIA: One moment, please.

> [GORKIN *and* VIKTOR *turn away and go into a huddle. They whisper urgently.* ZHIGALIN *leans forward and listens. While they do so:*]

It isn't a huge problem, is it, serving wine instead of vodka?

POINTER: We can't do it.

NADIA: Why not?

POINTER: Because we've just bought in two hundred bottles of vodka, that's why not.

> [GORKIN *and* VIKTOR *turn back to* POINTER *and* NADIA.]

GORKIN: Godspodin Pointer, ya bol'she nye v sostoyanii prodolzhat' etot spor.

NADIA: Mr. Pointer, I cannot continue with this argument.

GORKIN: ...potomu chto nye vizhu vozmozhnosti kompromisnovo ryesheniya.

NADIA: I can see no room for compromise.

GORKIN: Ya sovyetuyu vam obratit'sya k vyshestoyashchim organam s pros'boi dat' vam nyeobkhodimoye razryesheniye na zakupku vina.

NADIA: I suggest you go back to your superiors and obtain the necessary authority to order wine.

GORKIN: A syeichas mnye khotyelos' by pyeryeiti k
slyeduyushchemu punktu povyestki dnya...

NADIA: I should like to pass on to the next item on the
agenda...

GORKIN: ...to yest' — znachit — k voprosu o tyeatral'nom
spyektaklye.

NADIA: The visit to the theatre.

POINTER: Very well, Mr. Gorkin. I will see what can be done,
but I do not hold out much hope.

VIKTOR: ...nadyezhdy.

POINTER: We will discuss the matter again tomorrow
morning.

VIKTOR: ...zavtra utrom.

POINTER: Now then, the theatre.

VIKTOR: ...o spyektaklye.

POINTER: We received your message about the President's
tastes. We understand perfectly well that he doesn't
much like opera or ballet.

VIKTOR: ...ni opyeru, ni balyet.

POINTER: So, arrangements have been made for him to visit
our National Theatre, to see the excellent production of *Heartbreak House.*

VIKTOR: ...postanovku natsional'novo tyeatra *Heartbreak
House.*

GORKIN: No vyed' my vam soobshchili zaranyeye, chto i
Shekspir nye v yevo vkusye.

NADIA: But we told you, he doesn't like Shakespeare either.

POINTER: *Heartbreak House* is by George Bernard Shaw. [*to*
NADIA] Isn't it?

VIKTOR: ...Dzhordzh Byernard Sho.

GORKIN: My kak raz prosili komyediyu.

NADIA: We specified a comedy.

POINTER: *Heartbreak House* is a comedy. [*to* NADIA] Isn't it?

VIKTOR: ...komyediya.

[VIKTOR *whispers to* GORKIN.]

GORKIN: Nu, raz na etot shchyot sushchestvuyut somnyeniya,
my dolzhny provyerit' p'yesu.

NADIA: As there seems to be some doubt, we will have to vet
this play.

GORKIN: Nam nyemyedlyenno nuzhen tyekst.

NADIA: We must be given a copy immediately.

GORKIN: Vot nash Byelyayev govorit, chto on mozhet prochitat' p'yesu. My poslye etovo primyem sootvyetstvuyushcheye ryesheniye.

NADIA: Mr. Belaev here says he can read the play and then we will decide.

POINTER: [*plaintively*] But we've booked the tickets.

VIKTOR: ...bilyety.

POINTER: They're hard to come by.

VIKTOR: ...trudno...

POINTER: It's our National Theatre —

GORKIN: Nichevo nye popishesh'.

NADIA: That cannot be helped.

GORKIN: Nam nuzhen tyekst. Vy byeryotyes' eto obyespyechit'?

NADIA: We must have a copy. Can that be arranged?

GORKIN: V srochnom poryadkye.

NADIA: At once.

[POINTER *looks enquiringly at* NADIA.]

POINTER: Do you have a copy of *Heartbreak House*?

NADIA: Yes, but I don't carry it with me wherever I go.

VIKTOR: Could one be sent to me? Or, if that's too much trouble, I could collect it on my way back to the Embassy.

NADIA: I'm not sure I have a copy at my flat.

VIKTOR: Would you be so kind as to look? [*He smiles, oozing charm.*] I shall return it tomorrow. I promise. Miss — [*He consults a list and pronounces her name with difficulty.*] — Miss Ogilvie-Smith.

NADIA: [*confidentially to* POINTER] What do you think? Shall I oblige?

POINTER: Please. Anything that might help.

NADIA: [*to* VIKTOR] Very well. [*She writes on a piece of paper.*] I'll give you my address.

[*While she writes,* VIKTOR *has a quick word with* ZHIGALIN. GORKIN *takes leave of* POINTER.]

GORKIN: [*shaking hands with* POINTER] Do svidaniya.

NADIA: [*to* POINTER] It's really too tiresome; they behave like apes, then expect us to do favours for them.

ZHIGALIN: [*beaming for the benefit of all*] Yes. OK. I go shop. Go
shop.

> [*They all look at him, a little surprised by his
> intervention. Then* NADIA *hands her address to*
> VIKTOR.]

VIKTOR: [*reading*] Ennismore Gardens... Is that by the river?

NADIA: No. The Russian Orthodox Church.

> [*Blackout.*]

Lights reveal NADIA *entering the living room of her flat in
Ennismore Gardens: attractively furnished, yet distinctly
un-English. Many old family photographs in frames. Two
or three icons. There is a dining alcove.*

NADIA: [*calling*] Baboushka?

> [NADIA *hurriedly goes to the door, looks in, then
> quietly closes the door. She crosses to the bookcase
> and finds a copy of the play. The entryphone rings.*
> NADIA *crosses and picks up the receiver.*]

Yes? [*She listens.*] Come in.

> [*She presses the button that opens the front door of
> the building.*]

[*into the receiver*] Are you in?

> [*She opens the door of the flat. She puts her head
> out.*]

[*calling*] It's up here —

> [*She moves away.* VIKTOR *enters. He closes the door
> behind him. They stare at each other.*]

VIKTOR: Nadia, Nadia, I want you here, now.

> [*They kiss hungrily, violently. His hands seem to be
> everywhere.*]

NADIA: Oh my darling, Vitya, I've missed you —

VIKTOR: I want you now, now —

NADIA: Oh, Vitya, stop it. Oh, let go of me, this is so
dangerous —

> [VIKTOR *suddenly starts looking around the room.*]

There are no bugs in my flat, Viktor.

VIKTOR: You're sure?

NADIA: Positive.

VIKTOR: Then let me have you naked, let us both be naked —
      [*He starts to undress.*]

NADIA: Viktor, don't be a fool, my grandmother's asleep in the next room. She may wake up at any moment, please —
      [VIKTOR *is suddenly still, studying her, eyes narrowed.* NADIA *becomes more and more uneasy.*]

VIKTOR: What's happened to you?

NADIA: What do you mean what's happened to me?

VIKTOR: Ten years ago in New York we uncovered in each other a savage, barbaric passion which was utterly faithful to what we really are. Now you behave as if we're to begin all over again. What's happened?

NADIA: Viktor, *ten years* has happened —

VIKTOR: What has the passage of time to do with it?

NADIA: Viktor, I'm in a state of shock —

VIKTOR: Do you really not remember what we were to each other? In New York, we were barbarians —

NADIA: Yes, but this is Ennismore Gardens —

VIKTOR: For God's sake put aside that brittle English manner and come to me.

NADIA: I always thought it was my brittle English manner you loved so much —

VIKTOR: You *have* forgotten. I don't believe this, it's not possible to forget. We were two creatures with the appetites of barbarians —

NADIA: Do please stop using that word barbarian —

VIKTOR: Oh God, Nadia, I want to look down at you. I want to feel your hands on my back. I've never wanted anyone like I've wanted you.
      [NADIA *shivers uncontrollably.*]
Why are you quivering?

NADIA: I've been working terribly hard — I've worked very hard ever since — really one could say I've immersed myself — in work. I've been working ever since — Why did you leave so suddenly? You must have known you were being recalled, you should have warned me —

VIKTOR: I didn't. I swear I didn't, it was very sudden. But

that's all ancient history, just let me hold you, let us
be locked together —
> [NADIA *freezes, as if in pain, to ward him off. He
> bides his time.*]

NADIA: [*warning*] I'm fragile, Vitya. I haven't cried like this
for ages. Not for at least — was it really ten years
ago?

VIKTOR: You see, that's what I mean, time is meaningless.

NADIA: Ten years. Meaningless. Yes. Well. For ten
meaningless years I've had more or less to — I don't
tell many people this — I have a more or less
constant fight to keep — on an even keel. Sometimes, it's touch and go. People say, 'Time the great
healer', but I haven't found that to be true — I wish
I hadn't said that — I'm just particularly vulnerable
at the moment, that's understandable, isn't it?
Mostly I'm buoyant, but I plunge, I soar, literally
from moment to moment — it's just that today —
seeing you —
> [VIKTOR *holds her close. Silence for a moment.*]

VIKTOR: For ten years I've thought of nothing but this
embrace.

NADIA: I remember it all so — it seems like the day before
yesterday.

VIKTOR: You look the same. Only more lovely.

NADIA: You look younger.

VIKTOR: We had fun, didn't we?

NADIA: Did we?

VIKTOR: Oh yes, we did, we did. I remember so much laugh-
ter, so much fun —

NADIA: I don't remember any fun at all.

VIKTOR: If you don't remember any fun, why are you crying?
> [NADIA *moves away.*]
You invade my thoughts. Odd, stupid things I remember. I used to get so angry. I never understood
why you always laughed when I said the most serious things.

NADIA: I only laughed when I knew you were lying. You
lied all the time, that's why I always laughed.

VIKTOR: The way you could zip up a dress at the back without help. So ridiculous. God, life is cruel.

NADIA: [*laughing*] No, life isn't cruel, life is tragic. [*suddenly crying*] Life's a farce.

VIKTOR: Are you still doing those translations of Chekhov?

NADIA: [*through her tears*] Nyet. Dostoevsky.

VIKTOR: Do you really not remember the fun? I'm astonished. We had such an original, passionate romance, charged with high drama and political intrigue, extraordinary sensuality and delicious enjoyment. We eluded the security services of two great powers for almost eleven months. Well, one great power and yours. Wasn't that fun? And all those extraordinary and unique places we made love. Wasn't that fun? Oh God, I adored that, making love to you when and where you least expected it. You remember the time in the shower at the Italian Embassy and in the sea off Long Island, and behind the fountain at the Lincoln Centre, don't you remember?

NADIA: Yes, I remember that water made you uncontrollable. Or did it? Wasn't it just to amuse me? I never really believed a word you said. Please don't go on about it, it embarrasses me terribly — I can't believe we did what we did — I sometimes have these dreams, recurring dreams, of us in the water, I'm usually drowning but when I wake —

VIKTOR: [*tormented*] Oh, for God's sake, I can't bear this, let me have you on the floor, here, now, or better in the bathroom, with the taps running, your grandmother won't mind —

NADIA: She will, she will –

VIKTOR: [*almost as if in pain*] Will she really?

[NADIA *finds her handbag, takes out a compact and adjusts her appearance.*]

You never married?

[*No response.*]

Have you had lots of lovers?

[*No response.*]

How many?

[*No response.*]
You must have been horribly lonely.
[*No response.*]
You've had your work, of course — you said —

NADIA: [*suddenly flaring*] My work? You call what we did today work? That was disgraceful, Viktor. What did we talk about? Whether a man should drink vodka or wine? You call that work? God, I felt so helpless —

VIKTOR: Helpless, right.

NADIA: If my mind hadn't been reeling from seeing you again, I'd have stood up and told them to stop behaving like two waiters in a second-rate restaurant.

VIKTOR: And if we were speaking the truth, Stepanov wouldn't know Château Latour from the pee of the weasel. Don't let's talk about it. Let's only talk about things that really matter.

NADIA: We should have spoken out instead of sitting there, helpless, interpreting the inanities of grown-up half-wits. We're simply helpless, sometimes I have this almost uncontrollable desire —
[*She breaks off.*]

VIKTOR: Oh, Nadia, you are the most sensitive creature I have ever known. [*Pause.*] Helpless, yes, helpless.
[NADIA *gives in to her unhappiness. She seems drained.* VIKTOR *watches her, trying to control himself from taking hold of her.*]
Here's something to cheer you up. My wife divorced me.

NADIA: I'm not surprised.

VIKTOR: She'd had enough.

NADIA: I can believe that.
[*Pause.*]

VIKTOR: I wanted you, Nadia, for ten years I've wanted you, day, night, heart, soul, body, body —

NADIA: I heard you the first time —

VIKTOR: [*suddenly exploding with passion*] I want you now, now,

I want to undress you —

NADIA: Oh, Viktor, please stop torturing me —

VIKTOR: But it's you who are torturing me. [*He calms himself.*] I am not ashamed of my lust. I often think the acquisition of education and insights stifles our most valuable human feelings. Only with you, Nadia, have I ever known that ideal of emotional tenderness and sexual triumph. 'Come live with me and *be* my love. And we will many *pleasures* seek.' There you have it. Delicacy of feeling and the hope of sensual gratification. Did we not lie together in the aftermath of passion, listening to that music —

> [*He hums softly the 'Nimrod' theme from Elgar's Enigma Variations.* NADIA *weeps silently. He moves closer to her.*]

NADIA: I'd forgotten how cruel you could be.

VIKTOR: Yes, nothing provokes memory more potently than music. We sought pleasure and we found it. We can seek and find again. Come, let us reveal once more our true natures.

> [*They seem for a moment poised to come together. But* NADIA *turns away.*]

NADIA: Viktor, I've settled for a certain kind of — I live here in peace with my aged grandmother. It's the life I want for myself. I avoid turmoil. I daren't — I — did I tell you I went to pieces after you left New York? Not a real breakdown, I mean, not terribly serious but — I simply couldn't function for a bit. I mustn't make it sound worse than — but — well — I think one could describe it as painful. I made a conscious choice to live the way I do. It's what I want, and I take the consequences. Just the other day I overheard the Secretary of State say, 'The trouble with Nadia is that she's not getting it regular' —

VIKTOR: Getting it regular? Is that correct?

NADIA: Oh yes, it's correct, all right, I haven't — Oh, I see — No. It's a sort of slang. A joke.

VIKTOR: I never really understood your English jokes, I feel it
         to be a great lack. What does it mean, this irregu-
         larity?

NADIA: It means my male colleagues make passes at me
         which I rebuff. And that astonishes them. It never
         enters their heads it's because I find them colourless,
         clumsy and flaccid. They have to think it's because
         I'm frigid.

VIKTOR: You? Frigid? Are they insane?

NADIA: No, just English. But because they're desperate for
         it, they think I am. But I'm not. I am congenitally
         unable to give myself. I take the words 'making love'
         too literally. You learned that in New York. I don't
         mean to sound prudish. I'm simply telling you how I
         cope. Or at least, how I try to — [*brushing the thought
         aside*] And so to put it bluntly, the fact of the matter
         is that your very presence in this flat, in this country,
         endangers my existence. I daren't even contemplate
         what I feel for you.

VIKTOR: We fooled them for eleven months in New York, on
         dry land and in wet water. We can fool them for a
         few days in London. Nadia, please, be reasonable —
                  [*Humming the Elgar, he unzips her dress from the
                  back. She zips it up without assistance.*]
         I can't bear to watch you do that. It excites me
         inordinately. [*advancing on her*] Believe me, there's no
         danger, both our Security Services are incredibly
         stupid.

NADIA: I'm not talking about the Security Services. [*Pause.*]
         I'm not well equipped for love and jealousy or in-
         trigue and deception. They neither amuse nor
         stimulate me. The truth is I'm cowardly. I fear
         upheaval. That's what the doctor said — the shrink,
         that's an Americanism, like screw, so descriptive —
         I long for quietude. I want stability. I want my
         future to be unsurprising. I can't face another bat-
         tering. I have known one grand passion in my life.
         You. One can never go back. The only trace that
         exists of our affair is in us, or perhaps just in me, and

I am insignificant. I haven't the strength to resurrect the dead. Rest in peace.

VIKTOR: Beautiful Nadia, listen to me. I do not understand why a man should put in hazard his entire life for this woman or that woman, but for one particular woman, for you — I would endanger — I — [*He stops.*] Most people know nothing of such obsessions. Most people cannot imagine what it is like to be overwhelmed with this astonishing desire, this ache, this mental and physical excitation that ends either in ecstasy or despair. Let me ravish you. I am burning with passion. Let us be furtive, clumsy, let us be entwined. Let us be what we are. Lovers.

> [NADIA *turns away from him. He takes her and tries to kiss her. She holds him off.*]

NADIA: Viktor, my grandmother is in the next room.

VIKTOR: Your grandmother?

NADIA: You remember. I talked of her often. Tarasova. She's asleep in the next room.

> [VIKTOR *paces nervously.* NADIA, *too, is again dangerously on edge.*]

VIKTOR: Tarasova. Of course. She must be very old now.

NADIA: She's ninety-three.

VIKTOR: That's very old.

NADIA: Yes.

VIKTOR: She still dancing?

NADIA: [*irritated*] She's ninety-three, Viktor.

VIKTOR: The Ballets Russes.

NADIA: The Ballets Russes.

VIKTOR: She'll like my nanny, Zhigalin.

NADIA: Is he the ape that wanted to 'go shop'?

VIKTOR: Yes. He's KGB. His father was a ballet critic.

NADIA: She won't like him at all.

> [VIKTOR *stops pacing, suddenly realising something.*]

VIKTOR: She's ninety-three?

NADIA: Last May.

VIKTOR: Then, my God, we're fools. [*triumphant*] If she's ninety-three, she sleeps soundly.

[*He tries to grab her.*]

NADIA: [*pushing him away*] She also wakes suddenly.

[VIKTOR *rocks to and fro, as if in pain.*]

VIKTOR: Am I never to have you again? Even for the briefest moment?

NADIA: Go away, get out. Leave me in one piece. Haven't you understood? I don't want two or three days of sexual athletics only to be abandoned again, lacerated and helpless. My time is past for casual affairs, even with barbarians.

VIKTOR: Who's talking about casual affairs?

NADIA: You are — I don't approve — I never did. You know that — I don't approve of making love as though it were an oil change.

VIKTOR: [*suddenly furious*] How dare you? You think it gives me pleasure to be crude and impatient? You think in more amenable circumstances I wouldn't sit and talk and talk and talk until we had explored the mystery of our existence? Am I not Russian? You are not the only one that likes to woo, and screw. But I am hungry for you Nadia, and time is short. To be Russian needs eternity. I haven't that long. The Embassy will become suspicious. All I ask is that we lose ourselves in each other —

NADIA: I don't want to hear any more.

[*She hands him the copy of the play.*]

Please go. Take the play.

VIKTOR: Don't be silly. I know the play. I did my thesis in G.B. Shaw and H.G. Wells. It was just a ruse. A bally ruse.

[*He laughs delightedly at his own joke, and pockets the play.*]

NADIA: [*irritated*] It's not that funny. And I might have known. You can do nothing without deceit. If it's honest, it isn't fun. Please go. For both our sakes. I shall sit opposite you all day tomorrow and the next. I shall look longingly at you. I can't pretend I don't still find you — [*She stops herself.*] My eyes will fill with tears from time to time. But that's all. To

consider anything else would be futile. We have no
future. We never did.

[VIKTOR *becomes deadly still.*]

VIKTOR: I wish you hadn't said those words.

NADIA: What words?

VIKTOR: We have no future. I've squandered my life, never
stopping to think, saying yes to everything and anything, relying on all my hateful qualities to get me
through: my charm, my intelligence, my sex appeal,
my nervous energy. You are the only person I know
who has the power to throw me into such confusion
that I, who pride myself on my analytical mind,
cannot understand what is happening to me. I'm
going to make a confession, Nadia. I want your
word, as my friend if nothing else, that what I'm
about to say will die with you.

[*No response.*]

I have only been telling you half the truth.

NADIA: Let me guess: you only want half my body.

VIKTOR: Don't make light of this. What I am about to say is
deadly serious. A matter of life and death. My life
and death. After our affair in New York my career
was in the doldrums. I spent four or five years in the
Ministry of Ferrous Metallurgy. Doing translations.
Then I was sent on a mission to Istanbul. Our
Second Secretary there defected. He walked into
your Embassy and asked for political asylum. They
needed someone to interpret for our Ambassador.
They sent me. One afternoon, arguing with your
man there, Nightingale, his name was —

NADIA: I know him —

VIKTOR: I know you know him. That's the whole point of the
story. Nightingale asked me, while I was sitting
there, casually, whether I knew you. [*Pause.*] Just a
simple question like that. 'By the way,' he said, 'Do
you know Nadia Ogilvie-Smith?' And it was as if
you were there, as if I could touch you, smell you,
kiss you. Believe me, now, Nadia. This is the truth.
Sitting there in that small, stuffy office, the sweat

running down my face and back, I had such an
overwhelming desire to see you again, that I — that
I — that I wanted to defect —
[*Silence. Then* NADIA *laughs.*]
You see? You see? I make the most serious statement
of my life, and you laugh —
[NADIA *stops laughing.*]

NADIA: I only laugh when I know you're lying. Change the
subject, let's talk about real life.

VIKTOR: I swear to you I was about to ask Nightingale for
asylum when our Ambassador entered. The opportunity evaporated. But not the idea. Now, you know
I am an obsessive character, and I became obsessed
with this idea of leading the rest of my life with
you —

NADIA: Viktor, I prefer half truths to whole lies —

VIKTOR: Please don't interrupt. This is difficult for me. When
you said just now we had no future the earth opened
up and I dropped into a bottomless chasm. I was not
going to tell you my plans until much later. But I
have made a decision. At the end of the meetings.
Here. In London. It may be my last opportunity. I
am going to defect.

NADIA: [*fighting to keep calm*] I never heard that, Viktor. You
didn't say it, any of it. Perhaps you'd like to try
another approach. Only this time be a little more
sophisticated, give me credit for having some intelligence, not much, I know —

VIKTOR: Can't you recognise the truth when it stands up and
spits you in the eye? I love you. Love, worship,
adoration, desire, the whole panoply of human fas-
cination, one for another I feel for you. I do not
understand the borders between love and lust. I
know there is nothing easier than to say 'I love you'
in order to achieve disreputable ends. There is also
nothing more difficult than to make another believe
the words, I love you. But what other words are
there? I love you, believe me, glorious Nadia. I open

my heart to you, I lay before you my future life on this planet.

[*Pause.*]

What do you say?

NADIA: I don't want any more pain.

VIKTOR: [*gently*] Nadia, there is no life without pain, without movement. Sometimes violent movement. I want to spend the rest of my life with you and I am willing to sacrifice everything to make it come true. That is why I beg you to believe me, my darling, reckless woman. I am going to defect for love of you.

NADIA: What are you telling me? That you put me above country, party, ideology?

[VIKTOR *moves closer to her.*]

VIKTOR: Ideology? What ideology? There is no ideology but power, privilege, and personal well-being. In every country on earth. To hell with it all. The closer you get to power the more vile the stench. I've had enough. I choose human values above country, party and ideology. I choose you, Nadia —

[*He tries to kiss her. She holds him off.*]

NADIA: I don't trust you. I never did —

VIKTOR: But I've changed —

NADIA: Were you ever really in love with me, were you —?

VIKTOR: [*continuing, almost simultaneously*] I am convulsed by change, can't you see that?

NADIA: No, I can't —

VIKTOR: Nadia, I'm burning with sincerity —

NADIA: You're burning with something else, you're simply concupiscent.

VIKTOR: [*alert*] Please, what is this concupiscent? I don't know this word. What does concupiscent mean?

NADIA: Randy.

VIKTOR: Ah. This I cannot deny. [*He smiles.*] Concupiscent. Good.

NADIA: Every instinct in me screams out against you.

VIKTOR: How can you say that? How dare you say that?

NADIA: What about Olya Rashidova?

VIKTOR: [*alarmed*] Olya Rashidova?

NADIA: Yes, Olya Rashidova, your assistant at the UN. Have you forgotten her already? She told me you became engaged. You gave her a ring —

VIKTOR: Olya Rashidova told you that? Olya Rashidova? How could I become engaged to Olya Rashidova? She had a bushy Cossack moustache.

NADIA: She said you introduced her to everyone as your fiancée and it was two weeks before she found out you were already married.

[*Pause.*]

VIKTOR: No, no. You're right. I behaved badly. I should never have given her the ring.

NADIA: I'm not concerned about the ring. What about the lies? To Olya? To your wife?

VIKTOR: I never lied to my wife. I never told her about Olya.

NADIA: You are the most unscrupulous man that ever trod the earth.

[VIKTOR's *mood plummets.*]

VIKTOR: I cannot deny it. I'm a cad.

NADIA: You're a skunk.

VIKTOR: Yes. I'm disgusting. I despise myself.

NADIA: Oh, for God's sake stop that wallowing, I can't bear it.

VIKTOR: Allow me to enjoy my remorse just as you enjoy your suffering —

NADIA: I enjoy suffering? Ha!

VIKTOR: Of course you do. It's part of your inheritance. And mine. I sometimes behave vilely, always to those people I value most, and then I am crushed by remorse. I am utterly despicable.

NADIA: You're crushed by your own deceit. You're nothing more than a liar by conviction.

VIKTOR: This time you are wrong. I am going to defect.

[*He tries to take hold of her.*]

Believe me, I know the dangers. I know what you will have to go through, what we both will have to go through, the endless questions, suspicions, the prob-

ing. But I'll stand by you. We will be debriefed
together.

[NADIA *laughs.*]

I am speaking the truth, Nadia, we have to face the
future hand in hand. Will you help me, will you?

NADIA: You're not serious —

VIKTOR: Just listen, listen, I must get back to the Embassy.
What I need is a smokescreen. I have a thick im-
penetrable smokescreen. I have the beginnings of a
plan, confused, but taking shape —

NADIA: I don't want to hear —

VIKTOR: Could you give a party?

NADIA: Viktor!

VIKTOR: Could you give a party, here in your flat — ? We'll
ask everybody, your Mr. Pointer, my Mr. Gorkin,
Nanny Zhigalin, we'll get them very drunk and
afterwards —

NADIA: Viktor, stop, stop, stop! There is going to be no
party and you are not going to defect here in my
grandmother's flat —

VIKTOR: Nadia, why do you say that? You said you would
help —

NADIA: I never said anything of the kind.

VIKTOR: Your grandmother! Tarasova! Of course! That's excellent. I will use her as bait —

NADIA: Oh, no you won't —

VIKTOR: I'll talk to her, I promise you I get on very well with
old ladies. But the important thing is, Zhigalin
won't be able to resist her. He loves the ballet and
when he gets drunk he dances 'The Dying Swan'.

NADIA: He doesn't.

VIKTOR: Yes, I am afraid he does, he's really quite amusing.
And we shall get him very, very drunk —

NADIA: Not 'we' Viktor, not me, please, please, please, don't
involve me —

VIKTOR: But you are involved. I am doing all this for one
reason and one reason only: for you, Nadia. I am
going to defect for you.

NADIA: Are you serious? Don't be serious, please —
        [SOPHIA *enters.*]

SOPHIA: Nadia, extraordinary, I just dreamed in Russian.
        Imagine. I have not dreamed in this language since
        nineteen-hundred twenty-two. French, yes. English,
        of course. But Russian not. What you make of this?
        Death is near? Mystery force calling me back to land
        of birth? Premonition? Who knows? I forget dreams
        but I remember language. [*She sees* VIKTOR.] You
        have a guest. Apology. Who is this man?

NADIA: This is Viktor Belaev. This is my grandmother,
        Sophia Ogilvie-Smith.

VIKTOR: [*bowing*] Ochen' rad poznakomit'sya.

SOPHIA: [*cutting him short like ice*] I do not speak Russian. It is
        my form of protest. I have not spoken this language
        since November nineteen-hundred eighteen. And
        you do not speak Russian either. You speak Cock-
        ney. [*like a cat in pain; rapidly*] Miaow, miaow,
        miaow, miaow. [*She looks him over.*] Belaev, Belaev.
        Why I know that name? For Soviet you are almost
        beautiful. How old you think I am?

VIKTOR: [*after some consideration*] Seventy-five?

SOPHIA: Such much? I get new wig.

VIKTOR: No, no, it's charming. But Nadia, what is your deci-
        sion?

NADIA: I have to be persuaded you mean what you say —

SOPHIA: What is happening here? It could be a storm. I hear
        baying of wolf, and wind rising. [*to* VIKTOR] I have
        sixth sense. Other five useless. What you do here?

NADIA: Mr. Belaev is the Soviet interpreter. He's a friend of
        Mr. Stepanov.

SOPHIA: Stepanov is pig.

NADIA: Baboushka —

SOPHIA: I am an old woman. I speak my mind. How was
        meeting today? We declare war, I hope.

NADIA: Not quite, but it was a close-run thing.

SOPHIA: This I predict. With Bolsheviks business is fraud.
        Also with Americans. In Chicago contract, 1924,
        small print, immoral.

NADIA: Come and sit —

SOPHIA: How old do you think I am?

[VIKTOR *looks at* NADIA, *who shrugs.*]

Ninety-three. But admitting only eighty-nine. [*She laughs, more a wheeze than anything else.*] Yet. Faculties intact. Vocabulary does not include senility.

VIKTOR: That is perfectly obvious, Madam.

SOPHIA: Belaev, why you work for that pig Stepanov? Come. Talk to me. I see few people now. Nadia always here and there. All friends dead. I am an interesting woman. You know who I am?

VIKTOR: Of course. Nadia —

SOPHIA: I am Tarasova. That makes surprise for you. You think Tarasova dead. No. Here I am. I still do plié. With Nijinsky I dance, you know that? I am interesting woman.

VIKTOR: Of course. You are a household name, Madam. And I have colleagues who would simply adore to meet you, don't I, Nadia?

NADIA: Very likely, but they may have to be disappointed.

SOPHIA: Talk to me. I have known everyone of importance this century. I went to theatre with Tolstoy. You know who is Tolstoy?

VIKTOR: Of course —

SOPHIA: Chekhov, I meet — twice I meet Anton Pavlovich. Once with Tolstoy, other times two weeks before death in Badenweiller. Who else? Diaghilev, naturally, Nijinksy, unnaturally — [*She laughs.*] You know what this man, ah, what's his name, this man, oh God, I forget, you know what he is saying about me? He is saying, 'You name-drop on cosmic scale.' [*Pause.*] Stravinsky, that was him, Igor Fyodorovich Stravinsky. [*She chuckles, wheezes and coughs.*] I give up smoking soon. Tell me about yourself. You know my granddaughter, Nadia? Where is she?

NADIA: I'm here, Baboushka —

VIKTOR: Yes, she's here, Nadia why don't you join us, we've so much to discuss —

SOPHIA: Ah, Nadia, clever, beautiful, intelligent in all things, except love. In New York she have love affair with some low-down skunk. Cause much unhappiness.

NADIA: Baboushka, enough now. Mr. Belaev is just leaving.

VIKTOR: No, he's not.

SOPHIA: Belaev, why you work for this pig Stepanov?

VIKTOR: [*to* NADIA] I can't go until I know your answer.

SOPHIA: Talk to me. How old you think I am?

VIKTOR: Eighty-nine.

SOPHIA: Not bad.

VIKTOR: [*to* NADIA] Don't go.

[NADIA *exits.*]

SOPHIA: *Venez ici.* Let us gossip. I love gossip, sit by me.

[VIKTOR *sits uneasily.* SOPHIA *suddenly grabs his wrist and holds him in a claw-tight grip.*]

What is this disturbance? If you bring suffering, I destroy you.

VIKTOR: [*astonished*] I have no intention —

SOPHIA: Speak only truth to me. You think I am gaga. Think again. You know what old age brings? Not only decay but also divination. When physical life is empty, mental faculties increase. Wisdom, no, x-ray eyes, yes. I may only be ballerina but I smell in the air thunder. Something is not right. What?

VIKTOR: Nothing, Madam, I assure you —

SOPHIA: My Nadia is precious. She has true spiritual life, true human values. She has suffered. She has soul. You know this word soul?

VIKTOR: Yes.

SOPHIA: Oh, you give me surprise. I thought Bolsheviks abolished soul. I look at you, Belaev, and I make half-time report. You have soul — all Russians have soul — but you keep hidden. Why you do this? What game you play?

VIKTOR: No game, I promise —

SOPHIA: [*remembering*] Belaev, Belaev, I know this name. Yes! There was Belaev, corps de ballet, Ballets Russes, Monte Carlo. Scandal. In *Giselle.* This Belaev caught with second ballerina making unspeakable things. In swimming pool. I remember. She was

Queen of the Willis. [*Pause.*] This Belaev, any relation?

VIKTOR: It sounds possible. Madam, please let go of me —
> [SOPHIA *holds him. She is lost in thought. He tries
> gently to pull away.*

> *From the bathroom the sound of* NADIA *running her
> bath.*

> *The first sound of water running stills* VIKTOR,
> *then he smiles. He tries again to pull away.*]

SOPHIA: [*in her own world*] I was married to wonderful man.
Sir Julian Ogilvie-Smith. Only drawback his name.
Impossible to say. I ruined his career. He was diplomat. I am not diplomat. Our son, father of Nadia, is
banker, Hong Kong. Her mother run off with
Chinese pyschiatrist. Unhappy woman. Nadia has
much of her.
> [*Silence but for the running water.*]

I have question for you. Do you love lie or truth?
> [VIKTOR *extricates himself.* SOPHIA *doesn't seem to
> notice.* VIKTOR *rises. He edges nearer and nearer to
> the sound of the water.*]

Cards very interesting today.
> [*She studies them.* VIKTOR *darts off.* SOPHIA *gazes
> at the cards.*]

What you wish to prove, Belaev? You have too
much in you of this earth, Belaev. You want, you
hunger, you grab. You are Bolshevik. Not polite.
Not soulful. You are opportunist. Oh God, I am
fearful.
> [*Sound of splashing offstage.* SOPHIA *is unaware of
> anything but her own thoughts.*]

You are paradox, Belaev. Half lie, half truth. And,
Nadia? Let me see.
> [*She lays out more cards. The splashing continues
> offstage. Then, silence.*]

Nadia, Nadia, nothing but confusion. She is not yet
born. [*Pause.*] There is only one human virtue: abil-
ity to tell truth. Truth, my God, difficult subject.

You know what is truth? Never speaking lie. [*She
laughs, sneezes and coughs.*] This is paradox. Truth is
never speaking lie. I like this. [*Pause.*] Oh, God. I
smell in the air electrical storm.

> [VIKTOR *returns, soaking wet, beaming.* SOPHIA
> *turns to him.*]

Is raining already?

> [VIKTOR *cannot stop grinning. Impulsively, he cros-*
> *ses to* SOPHIA *and kisses her on the cheek.*]

VIKTOR: Madam, we will meet again. In a couple of days.
You're going to come to the party. Thank you. I am
so happy.

> [*He gets his coat and hat. He goes.*]

SOPHIA: You are insane. I have not been to party for twenty
years. What party?

> [*She quickly lays out another row of cards.* NADIA
> *runs in. She wears a towelling dressing-gown.*]

NADIA: Vitya? Vitya? Has he gone?

SOPHIA: I see no party. Only, I see — can this be right?
Nadia, Nadia, take care —

NADIA: Ach, Baboushka, what have I done? I've put my life
in hazard. [*She breaks off.*] I'm so happy, I don't
know whether to laugh or cry. One moment I was
saying I wanted no upheaval, the next, the world
has turned upside down. Isn't life extraordinary?
Isn't it unpredictable and glorious and unsettling? I
hadn't realised how much I longed for him. I am
enriched. I am intoxicated. I am happy.

> [*She kisses* SOPHIA *and runs off.* SOPHIA *studies the*
> *cards.*]

SOPHIA: Happy, happy, what is this *idée fixe* with happy?
Where is gone suffering? [*She studies the cards again.*]
Jack and Queen of Hearts. Two kings, Spades and
Diamonds. What means this? How to interpret? [*She
becomes suddenly alarmed then genuinely frightened.*] My
God, the skunk —

> [*Blackout.*]

ACT TWO

Light on NADIA, *wearing dark glasses.*

NADIA: At that moment, I believe I was happy. Although I confess the pursuit of happiness has always seemed to be foolhardy, futile, not to say illusory. Who was that Russian who said, 'If we were meant to be happy, there'd be no death'?

[*She squeezes a smile.*]

That's a Russian joke, you know. However, the heart of the matter, now that I look back, is not a question of happiness. The question you will want answered is, did I believe Viktor Belaev? Did I believe in his whirlwind of promiscuity, passion and promises? Did I really believe he would defect for love of me? Did I want him to? Did I encourage him? To the last, at least, I can answer yes. I encouraged him. Being — how shall I put it? — cognisant of his predilections, the running of water may be properly regarded as a mating-call. I knew what I was doing. I am ashamed of my own crudeness. But these were games he and I had played before. And playing them again revived my frail spirits. This is my interpretation. Mr. Belaev may, of course, have a different view. And there was danger. We were both, I suspect, unduly stimulated by danger. That may be a clue. Because what I did next was dangerous all right, truly, thoughtlessly, dangerous.

Lights grow. NADIA *walks into the Conference Room.*

GORKIN, *grim-faced, and* VIKTOR *sit on one side of the table.* NADIA *takes her seat beside* POINTER *on the opposite side of the table. From the moment she sits,* NADIA *has eyes only for* VIKTOR, *and he for her.*

POINTER: Mr. Gorkin, yesterday we seemed to get tangled up over what may be described as peripheral matters.

VIKTOR: ...vchera kak-budto vyshla u nas putanitsa.

POINTER: I thought that today we might try again to see if we can reach some compromise.

VIKTOR: ...syevodnya dobit'sya kompromisa.

POINTER: However, I am bound to say...

VIKTOR: ...ya dolzhen skazat'...

POINTER: ...that when it was known that His Excellency, President Stepanov, had agreed to visit...

VIKTOR: ...soglasilsya posyetit'...

POINTER: ...the United Kingdom...

VIKTOR: ...Korolyevstvo...

POINTER: ...certain arrangements were made by us...

VIKTOR: ...prinyali myeropriyatiya...

POINTER: ...to ensure the President's comfort and enjoyment.

VIKTOR: ...dlya udobstva Pryezidyenta.

POINTER: [*continuing with finality and some reluctance*] And those arrangements included certain provisions to which we are now tied.

GORKIN: I, naskol'ko ya ponimayu, eto, znachit, budyet vodka, a nye vino.

NADIA: And that, I take it, means vodka, not wine.

POINTER: [*a half-hearted smile*] Exactly. Vodka, not wine.

VIKTOR: ...vodka, nye vino.

GORKIN: [*stern, unrelenting*] Ya khotyel by yeshcho raz napomnit' vam o tom, chto govoril v etoi svyazi vchera.

NADIA: [*eyes on* VIKTOR, *mischievous; apparently translating*] I'm going to give you all the help I can.

GORKIN: Nasha pozitsiya vam khorosho izvyestna.

NADIA: [*apparently translating*] I was in a difficult mood yesterday.

GORKIN: Khochu podcherknut', chto ona ostayotsya nyeizmyennoi.

NADIA: ...but today I feel magnanimous.
        [*Stunned silence.*]

POINTER: [*to* NADIA] Did you get that absolutely right?

NADIA: [*to* VIKTOR] Did I, Mr. Belaev?

GORKIN: [*wagging his finger threateningly*] Eto chto takoye? Pryedupryezhdayu, chto v sluchaye umyshlyennovo iskazheniya moikh slov, nami budut sdyelany sootvyetstvuyushchiye vyvody.

NADIA: [*apparently translating*] I warn you I'm quite a different man when the sun is shining and enchantment is in the air.

GORKIN: My zdyes' nye byezzashchitny.

NADIA: [*apparently translating*] Life is beautiful.

POINTER: Well, I'm greatly encouraged.

VIKTOR: ...ya tak rad.

POINTER: I think this is the moment then to say...

VIKTOR: Yesli tak, to znachit, mogu skazat'...

POINTER: ...that I've discussed the matter and I'm afraid it's going to have to be vodka.

VIKTOR: ...k sozhalyeniyu obyezatyel'no vodka.

GORKIN: Nyet, nyet, nyet!

POINTER: I take that to mean 'no'.

NADIA: Up to a point.

POINTER: Up to a point?

VIKTOR: [*jumping in*] Miss Ogilvie-Smith is perfectly right. Nyet, nyet, nyet, is only 'no' up to a point. In Russian so much depends on the inflection.

POINTER: Really? [*to* GORKIN] You learn something every day.

VIKTOR: Vyek zhivi, vyek uchis'.

POINTER: How encouraging. Very well.

VIKTOR: Ochen' khorosho.

POINTER: I am bound to say, then, that we — we insist that at the Prime Minister's dinner, vodka is served throughout the meal.

VIKTOR: [*apparently translating*] ...ya gotov poiti na ustupki.
[GORKIN *listens to* VIKTOR's *translation. His face breaks into a huge grin.*]

GORKIN: Ladno. Khorosho.

NADIA: Good, good.

GORKIN: Raz vy gotovy poiti na ustupki, to i ya konyechno gotov vas vnimatyel'no slushat'.

NADIA: If you're willing to make concessions, I'm perfectly willing to listen.

POINTER: [*sharply to* NADIA] Concessions? I said nothing about concessions. [*to* GORKIN] Excuse me.[*to* NADIA] Are you sure you're getting this right? Let me have a look.

NADIA: What do you have, Mr. Belaev?
GORKIN: [*to* VIKTOR] Nu ka, ty, provyer'.
           [NADIA *and* VIKTOR *compare notes.*]
           Vsyo v poryadkye? Khorosho. [*to* POINTER] Davaitye
           pryamikom. Tak vot...
NADIA: Let's get down to basics. Here's the deal.
GORKIN: Khotitye, chtoby podavali zakuski i vodku? Idyot.
           No tol'ko v samom nachalye obyeda.
NADIA: You want to serve vodka and zakuski. OK. But only
           to begin with.
GORKIN: Vsyo ostal'noye vryemya budyet vino.
NADIA: For the rest of the meal, you serve wine.
GORKIN: Po rukam?
NADIA: How's that?
POINTER: [*relieved, but trying not to show it*] I shall certainly
           consider your suggestion and perhaps give you an
           answer tomorrow.
VIKTOR: ...na eto otvyechu zavtra.
POINTER: Nevertheless, I do feel we are moving towards a
           position we can both live with.
VIKTOR: ...dobit'sya soglasheniya.
POINTER: But, and I'm afraid there is another but, we have to
           draw the line at Château Latour and Château Mar-
           gaux.
                      [GORKIN *listens to the translation expressionlessly
                      but while* VIKTOR *translates* NADIA *slips off her
                      shoe and reaches out her foot. Gently, she strokes*
                      VIKTOR's *leg. He tries not to react.*]
VIKTOR: ...chto kasayetsya Shato Latur i Shato Margo.
                      [VIKTOR, *too, slips off a shoe. His and* NADIA's *feet
                      caress.*]
GORKIN: [*banging the table aggressively*] Vy chto, vsyo yeshcho
           prodolzhayetye stavit' pryedvarityel'nyye usloviya?
NADIA: [*apparently translating*] You see how easy it is to make
           progress?
POINTER: If this is progress...
VIKTOR: Yesli eto po-vashemu progryes...
POINTER: ...why are you banging the table in that objection-
           able way?

VIKTOR: ...tak b'yotye po stolu?

GORKIN: [*beaming*] Yasnosti radi.

NADIA: For emphasis.

POINTER: We certainly intend to serve two wines. A white with the fish course, of course... [*He smiles.*] ...and red with roast beef, Yorkshire pudding, roast potatoes, cabbage, peas, gravy, and horseradish sauce. It's exactly the same menu we served the President of the United States last year. Apart from the vodka and zakuski, naturally. As to the wines themselves, what would you say to — oh, I don't know... [*He glances at a paper.*] — a very jolly little Riesling, not Yugoslav, of course, and a really rather disarming Spanish Rioja?

> [NADIA *strokes* VIKTOR'*s foot, then crosses her leg, misses him and, by mistake, strokes* GORKIN. *He is at first astonished. Then he begins to leer.*]

Are you in agreement with that, Mr. Gorkin?

> [GORKIN *continues to leer at* NADIA.]

VIKTOR: ...vy soglasny?

POINTER: Mr. Gorkin?

GORKIN: Soglasyen.

NADIA: Yes, agreed.

> [VIKTOR *rises to get himself some water.* NADIA *continues to stroke* GORKIN, *then realises her mistake.* GORKIN *ends up holding* NADIA'*s shoe, which she quickly takes from him.* VIKTOR *and* NADIA *resume their former positions.*]

POINTER: Well, well. If you will trust us on the menu and the wine list, that's more than I — that's perfectly agreeable, of course.

VIKTOR: ...konyechno soglasyen.

POINTER: Fine, fine.

VIKTOR: Khorosho.

POINTER: I am absolutely delighted.

VIKTOR: Ya voskhishchyon.

POINTER: I make no secret of that. Now, what about dear old *Heartbreak House?*

VIKTOR: ...o p'yesye *Heartbreak House?*

POINTER: I took the trouble to read it last night and, I don't know about you, Mr. Belaev, but I thoroughly enjoyed it.

VIKTOR: ...ona mnye ochen' ponravilas'.

POINTER: It is, of course, a mixture of styles, but that's the point, isn't it? And some of it made me laugh out loud.

VIKTOR: ...prosto rassmyeyalsya.

POINTER: But I do want to say — and I think this is frightfully important, especially as far as President Stepanov is concerned — that the sub-title is "A fantasia in the Russian manner on English themes".

VIKTOR: ..."Fantazia na russki manyer po angliskim tyemam".

POINTER: Now, that really ought to satisfy everybody, what?
[He beams.]

GORKIN: K chortu tyeatr, gospodin Pointer.

NADIA: Mr. Pointer, to hell with the theatre!

GORKIN: Pochemu zhe vsye eti gosudarstvennyye glavy dolzhny pryedstavlyat' syebya takimi uzh kul'turnymi?

NADIA: Why do Heads of State always have to appear so cultured?

POINTER: Are you saying you don't want him to go to the theatre?

VIKTOR: ...nye khotitye, chtob on posyetil spyektakl'?

GORKIN: Da konyechno on obyazan posyetit' tyeatr. No, kakaya budyet p'yesa — naplyevat'!

NADIA: Of course he has to go to the theatre. But any play will do.

GORKIN: A na slyeduyushchem zasyedanii nyeobkhodimo budyet obsudit' vopros o tom, kto budyet vstryechat' tovarishcha Styepanova v aeroportu.

NADIA: At our next session I would like to talk about who's going to meet Mr. Stepanov at the airport.

GORKIN: Myezhdu prochim, smyeyu vas zavyerit', Mister Pointer...

NADIA: And I assure you, Mr. Pointer...

GORKIN: ...chto, vyidya iz samolyota, on nye stanyet, kak papa rimskii, tsyelovat' vashu zyemlyu.

NADIA: ...that when he arrives he won't kiss the ground like the Pope.

GORKIN: K Soyedinyonnomy Korolyevstvu on nikakikh pryetyenzi nye pitayet.

NADIA: He has no territorial designs on the United Kingdom.

POINTER: I am relieved to hear it.

VIKTOR: ...ochen' rad.

POINTER: But if he does kiss the ground, I may think he has turned Catholic.

            [*He laughs.*]

VIKTOR: ...mogu podumat', chto on pyeryeshyol v katolichestvo.

            [GORKIN *does not laugh.*]

Lights fade. POINTER *comes forward. Light on* POINTER.

POINTER: As I need hardly point out to members of this inquiry, in our world nothing is trivial. After that meeting, I was summoned to the office of the Assistant Under-Secretary. My deliberations with Mr. Gorkin had, of course, been monitored. Present in the office was a member of the Research Department. It was he who explained that Miss Ogilvie-Smith had made rather free translations of what Mr. Gorkin had said. At first, those listening in were amused, not to say admiring of her enterprise. But they became seriously worried when Belaev aided and abetted her, misinterpreting my words with equal abandon. They realised the two of them must be in league for reasons that were not yet clear. The Minister and I agreed to authorise surveillance of the two interpreters as a matter of urgency. It soon became clear that Mr. Belaev, with Miss Ogilvie-Smith's willing co-operation, intended to defect. Reports indicated that he would make his move after a party to be given by Miss Ogilvie-Smith at the end of our meetings, a party at which he planned to render a member of the Soviet delegation, Mr. Zhigalin, incapable. The implications were alarming. If

Belaev was to defect, the visit of Stepanov would be seriously compromised, if not cancelled altogether. Politically, that could not be entertained. I discussed the matter with the A.U.S., with the Head of my Department, and others. Various options were considered. In the end, we agreed upon a plan of action.

Lights grow.

POINTER *walks into* NADIA's *flat.*

ZHIGALIN, VIKTOR *and* GORKIN *are singing a Russian song.*

Also present are NADIA *and* SOPHIA.

The dining-table in the alcove is littered with the remains of zakuski. There are also two or three bottles of vodka in an ice-bucket, and other bottles of vodka around the room.

When the song finishes, NADIA, *in a highly charged state, claps too enthusiastically.* SOPHIA, *sipping vodka and smoking, is in her own world.* POINTER *drinks little and just listens.* GORKIN *stares with great intensity at* NADIA. *His mood is sullen.*

ZHIGALIN *stands before* SOPHIA *and bows low.*

ZHIGALIN: Tarasova, Tarasova —

> [VIKTOR *seems to fight emotion.* NADIA *draws* VIKTOR *aside.* GORKIN *watches them like a hawk.* ZHIGALIN *helps himself to vodka.*]

NADIA: [*urgently, referring to* ZHIGALIN] Zhigalin's no more drunk now than he was half an hour ago —

VIKTOR: Stop being so irritating. It'll happen, I will make certain it happens —

NADIA: But when, when? He must have consumed three bottles already.

VIKTOR: He'll pass out suddenly, he always does. Please, Nadia, relax. I am in control of the situation. You'll give the whole game away. I assure you, he's on the point of collapse.

> [*Suddenly, with whoops and shouts,* ZHIGALIN *breaks into a lively, Russian dance. He falls on his back and lies still.*]

NADIA: You were right. He's passed out.

[ZHIGALIN *suddenly jumps to his feet.*]

ZHIGALIN: Good party, good party!

[*He crosses to the alcove to refill his vodka glass.* NADIA *catches* POINTER'*s eye. She goes to him. Her manner is unnaturally cheerful.* VIKTOR *slides over, as if to keep an eye on her.*]

NADIA: [*to* POINTER] Isn't it extraordinary? Who'd have thought, two days ago, we'd have anything to celebrate?

POINTER: Who'd have thought?

NADIA: Are you pleased with us at the Office, Richard? I hope they're pleased with us. We got almost everything we wanted, didn't we? Vodka, Rioja and *Heartbreak House.* Look, look, how happy everyone is —

POINTER: Our masters are never happy.

NADIA: And you, Richard, are you happy? Have you had enough to eat, to drink, there's masses more —

POINTER: I'm fine, thank you. But if I'd known how these fellows put it away, I needn't have worried about the two hundred bottles of vodka.

[NADIA *forces a laugh.*]

NADIA: You're obviously happy. Excuse me —

[*She pours herself a drink and downs it. She hovers near the alcove.*]

SOPHIA: Mr. Pointer, *parlez avec moi.* No one talks to me any more. They think I'm dead.

POINTER: I'm sure that's not true.

[*He sits by* SOPHIA. *She studies him. He becomes uncomfortable.*]

SOPHIA: Why you not declare war on Soviet Union?

POINTER: Because it's just a little risky —

SOPHIA: We British become very cowardly.

[VIKTOR *approaches.*]

VIKTOR: Farewells are the saddest things in life.

SOPHIA: Ah, Belaev, so you are here.

VIKTOR: At your service, Madam.

[*He pours* SOPHIA *a drink.*]

SOPHIA: And, tell me, Belaev, what is your passion?

VIKTOR: My passion?

> [*He flicks a glance at* NADIA.]

SOPHIA: Ballet, literature, opera?

VIKTOR: [*considering*] Opera.

POINTER: That's the one when they sing to music.

VIKTOR: [*icy smile*] Yes, I know. In truth, I have a great passion for Britten.

> [POINTER *looks at him sharply; a sweeter smile.*]

Benjamin Britten. And Edward Elgar. And that British composer with the most heavenly of names, Arthur Bliss. I don't know any of his music but his name is very beautiful, Arthur Bliss.

NADIA: [*from the alcove*] And let's not forget Handel's *Water Music*.

GORKIN: Chto eto ty tam s nimi obsuzhdayesh'?

NADIA: Mr. Gorkin asks what are we discussing.

VIKTOR: [*to* GORKIN] Muzyku, Lyev Konstaninovich.

GORKIN: Voobshchye-to na zanadye muzyka sluzhit intyeresam razlagayushchyeisya burzhyazii.

VIKTOR: Mr. Gorkin says all western music is only for the decadent bourgeoisie.

POINTER: Oh, please tell Mr. Gorkin not to condemn the bourgeoisie. It's very old-fashioned of him.

> [VIKTOR *translates but* GORKIN *gestures that he doesn't want to hear.*]

It's been said, I can't remember the exact words but the burden of it was that when a nation gets rid of its bourgeoisie, terrible things occur. You have only to look at Nazi Germany and — [*slight pause*] — one or two other places. In this country, there would be no theatres or concert halls, or opera houses or art galleries if it weren't for the bourgeoisie. In England, if culture were left to the aristocrats and the working class, we'd have nothing but horse racing and homing-pigeons. So, please, please, beg Mr. Gorkin not to condemn the bourgeoisie.

> [NADIA *interrupts* VIKTOR*'s translation.*]

NADIA: [*to* VIKTOR] I'm going to do for him.

VIKTOR: Who? Who?

NADIA: Zhigalin.

VIKTOR: What d'you mean, do for him? Nadia, he's KGB, don't interfere. What are you going to do?

NADIA: I shall do what my grandmother taught me to do at the age of twelve: drink him under the table.

[ZHIGALIN *lurches towards her.*]

Davaitye vyp'yem, Boris Borisovich.

ZHIGALIN: Maximum woman. Drink. Yes. I like drink.

[*They fill their glasses.*]

NADIA: Her Majesty the Queen.

ZHIGALIN: Queen!

[*They drink and refill.*]

Nikolai Leonidovich Stepanov!

NADIA: Stepanov.

[*They drink. Their bottle is now empty. They retire to the alcove for reinforcements and continue to exchange toasts.*

VIKTOR, *vodka bottle in hand, goes to fill* POINTER'*s and* SOPHIA'*s glasses.*]

SOPHIA: [*to* VIKTOR] Belaev, you are tonight different.

VIKTOR: I? No. I'm always the same, Madam.

SOPHIA: No. Tonight, you are calm. Why?

POINTER: [*dryly*] I expect it's because he's happy.

VIKTOR: You're right, that's the reason, I'm happy.

[*He embraces* POINTER, *who pushes him off.*]

POINTER: Please, don't do that.

VIKTOR: You don't like affection?

POINTER: I don't like ostentation.

NADIA: The President of the United States.

ZHIGALIN: No, another.

NADIA: The President of the United States.

ZHIGALIN: OK. President.

SOPHIA: Why are you so happy, Belaev?

VIKTOR: The meetings have gone well, extraordinarily well. Nadia and I did a splendid job. I feel satisfied. Yes, I feel extremely satisfied.

ZHIGALIN: [*toasting*] Lyev Konstantinovich!

NADIA: Lyev Konstantinovich!

[*They drink, then open another bottle.*]

VIKTOR: I feel that we, Nadia and I, made a contribution, not simply as interpreters, but more important, as people, as individuals. So much more was accomplished. Don't you think?

POINTER: Absolutely. Mr. Gorkin and I agreed three whole menus in two days.

          [*He smiles.*]

VIKTOR: Sometimes one is inclined to feel — to feel —

POINTER: Helpless?

VIKTOR: Exactly, helpless, crushed by the weight of government, protocol, power. These days were different.

POINTER: Oh, very different.

ZHIGALIN: [*toasting*] Viktor Ivanovich Byelyayev!

NADIA: Viktor Ivanovich!

VIKTOR: And then, this is something you may not understand, Mr. Pointer, but I believe Sophia Ivanovna — I believe she will understand. I feel that we are all one here. Sophia Ivanovna, Nadia, me, Gorkin and Zhigalin. We are all Russians, the last people on earth capable of the highest feelings.

SOPHIA: And lowest deeds.

NADIA: [*toasting*] Mr. Pointer!

ZHIGALIN: Mr. Pointer!

VIKTOR: I am at peace in this apartment. Such an attractive room. These photographs, the samovar, the clock, the icons. How I miss icons. Well, of course, we still have them, only instead of the saints we have the Politburo. I look at this room, at you, Sophia Ivanovna, and I could cry for a vanished past. Such soulfulness in this day and age, in this place. I am always moved when the inner life is unexpected.

SOPHIA: Thank you. But you are not Russians. You are Soviets —

VIKTOR: We are people, individuals —

SOPHIA: Anton Pavlovich, he was Russian.

POINTER: Which Anton Pavlovich?

SOPHIA: Chekhov, Chekhov.

NADIA: [*toasting*] Chekhov!

ZHIGALIN: Chekhov!

SOPHIA: I knew him. Poor Anton Pavlovich.

POINTER: Why poor Anton Pavlovich?

SOPHIA: Why, because one time, when I am eleven years old, I go to theatre with Tolstoy. Tolstoy, family friend, take young person to theatre. Very nice. Play by Chekhov. *Swan Lake*, no?

POINTER: No. Chekhov didn't write *Swan Lake* —

SOPHIA: Sure, sure, *Swan Lake*, play with bird —

VIKTOR: *The Seagull. Chaika.*

SOPHIA: *Chaika,* you are right. *Seagull.* After play, Tolstoy take me to meet Chekhov. You know what says Tolstoy? He says, 'Anton Pavlovich, Shakespeare's plays are bad, but yours are worse.' Poor Anton Pavlovich, poor Anton Pavlovich.

ZHIGALIN: [*toasting*] My mistress, Galina Ilyinishna!

NADIA: Galina Ilyinishna!

> [GORKIN *sits apart from the others. He indulges now in a curious habit: using the thumb and little finger of his right hand as if they were a gun sight, he lines them up with the toe of his shoe.* VIKTOR, POINTER *and* SOPHIA *watch him.*]

VIKTOR: Look at Lev Konstantinovich. Isn't that Russian? What other nation could produce a high-ranking diplomat who is thinking of shooting himself in the foot?

POINTER: [*a faint smile*] I'm sure I could name one if I tried.

ZHIGALIN: [*toasting*] My wife, Maria Semyonovna!

NADIA: Maria Semyonovna. You swine.

> [*They drink.*]

ZHIGALIN: Your turn, your turn —

NADIA: [*in desperation*] The BBC World Service.

ZHIGALIN: BBC!

> [*They drink.*]

POINTER: [*to* SOPHIA] Oughtn't they to be smashing their glasses in the fireplace or somewhere?

SOPHIA: Absolute not. Only in American films they break glasses. In Russia, aristocrats drink much vodka. This is expensive. If also they break glasses, who could afford?

[*Each holding an empty bottle,* NADIA *and* ZHIGA-
LIN *leave the alcove.*]

ZHIGALIN: What please is name your father?

NADIA: Roland.

[ZHIGALIN *puts his hands on* NADIA*'s shoulders and
looks her in the eye.* GORKIN *is at once alert.*]

ZHIGALIN: Roland. Roland. OK. Nadyezhda Rolandovna, you
are fine fellow!

[*He embraces* NADIA. GORKIN *steps in between
them.*]

GORKIN: [*angrily and noisily rebuking* ZHIGALIN] Ty, Zhigalin!
Lapy proch' ot khozyaiki! Ponyal? Eto tyebye zdyes'
nye bordak! Proch'! Siyu minutu! Khochesh', ya
tyebya poshlyu po izvyestnomu adryesu!

[POINTER *moves surreptitiously closer to* VIKTOR
and NADIA.]

NADIA: I think I'm going to scream —

VIKTOR: It won't be long now, I promise. Soon, soon, our
lives will begin.

NADIA: I'm so utterly terrified, I'm going to scream —

VIKTOR: [*soothing her*] Nothing can stop us now. We will live
together in peace. I have nothing but love in my
heart. Even for myself. I have never liked myself,
Nadia. But tonight, tonight I feel I am turning over
a new page in my life, a new beginning, as though I
am entering the kingdom of heaven on earth.

NADIA: [*noticing* POINTER] Richard, would you like a drink?

POINTER: I have one over there —

VIKTOR: Life is beautiful. Tonight, when it is all over, and we
lie in each other's arms, we will allow ourselves at
least to dream of happiness.

NADIA: Why, when you talk like that, do I become more
frightened than ever?

VIKTOR: If I could kiss you here, I would kiss you —

[ZHIGALIN *begins to hum and dance 'The Dying
Swan'. It is comic and sad, grotesque and graceful.*]
[*quietly to* NADIA] Not long now.

[*They all watch* ZHIGALIN *dance.*]
[*to* SOPHIA] Isn't he amusing?

SOPHIA: Secret policeman dancing does not make me laugh.

VIKTOR: Don't poison the party, Sophia Ivanovna.

SOPHIA: There is only one Party I should like to poison.

> [*She rises and leaves the room with slow, deliberate dignity.* ZHIGALIN *reaches for her.*]

ZHIGALIN: Tarasova, Tarasova —

> [*And he collapses with the final shudder of the swan.* VIKTOR *goes to him and tries to lift him.*]

VIKTOR: I must get him back to the Embassy immediately. [*to* GORKIN] Pomogitye, Lyev Konstantinovich.

> [GORKIN *ignores him.* POINTER *helps* VIKTOR *lift* ZHIGALIN. NADIA *watches anxiously.* GORKIN *takes the opportunity to sidle up to* NADIA. *He whispers in her ear. He strokes her leg with his foot.*]

NADIA: [*turning on him*] Nye smyeitye trogat' myenya!

> [GORKIN *turns away and then helps* VIKTOR *and* POINTER *get* ZHIGALIN *to the door.* VIKTOR *so works it that* ZHIGALIN *hangs on to the others.*]

VIKTOR: Goodnight, goodnight, thank you for a wonderful party. Until tomorrow at the airport —

> [*He turns back to look at* NADIA *and purses his lips in a kiss.*]

NADIA: [*whispering*] Don't be long. Please, don't be long.

> [VIKTOR *and* GORKIN *exit with* ZHIGALIN *and* POINTER.
>
> *Alone,* NADIA *is still, frozen.*
>
> *The clock strikes one.* NADIA *does not move.*
>
> *The entry phone rings.* NADIA *rushes to it, presses the button and waits.*
>
> *A knock on the door.* NADIA *opens it.*
>
> VIKTOR *stands there, bleeding from the nose.* NADIA *goes towards him but* POINTER *and* GORKIN *appear.* GORKIN *nurses his hand. The three enter.*]

Oh, Richard, it's you. Have you forgotten something? Your hats, did you have hats? I don't see any hats — or umbrellas, was it umbrellas? — [*giving way to concern for* VIKTOR] Viktor, you're bleeding —

POINTER: [*icily*] That's because Mr. Gorkin hit him.

NADIA: [*barely audible*] Viktor, what's happened?

POINTER: [*to* VIKTOR*: a warning*] I'll do the talking. [*to* NADIA]
            We got Zhigalin into the car. There were angry
            words, shoving and pushing. Perhaps Belaev was
            trying to run away. Impossible to be certain. Mr.
            Gorkin insisted on coming back here. I agreed, be-
            cause we both need to keep the lid on this. For the
            moment. It's a joint operation. We know Belaev
            intends to defect.

VIKTOR: [*to* NADIA] Would you be so kind as to get me a drink,
            just water, and something for my nose? —
                        [NADIA *runs from the room.*]
            [*urgently: to* POINTER] Please, get another interpreter.
            I have some things to say that —

GORKIN: [*fiercely*] Ty, syad'! S tyebya bol'shye ni slova po-
            angliiski!

POINTER: What did Mr. Gorkin say?

VIKTOR: He doesn't want me to speak in English. I implore
            you —
                        [NADIA *returns with a cloth and a glass of water.*
                        She hands them to VIKTOR.]

POINTER: As soon as you're ready, Mr. Belaev. [*with a curt nod*]
            Thank you, Nadia.
                        [*They now arrange themselves so that* VIKTOR *and*
                        GORKIN *are side by side, close together in order that*
                        VIKTOR *can talk intimately to him.* NADIA *moves to*
                        her writing table to collect her note-book and pencil.]

VIKTOR: Ya nikogda nye khotyel byezhat', Lyev Konstan-
            tinovich...

POINTER: [*interrupting*] No. Wait, Mr. Belaev.
                        [POINTER *waits for* NADIA *to take her place.*]
            Right, Mr. Belaev.

VIKTOR: Ya nikogda nye khotyel byezhat', Lyev Konstan-
            tinovich. Vy ponyali vsyo sovyershenno nyevyerno.

NADIA: [*in a flat, unemotional voice*] I never intended to defect,
            Lev Konstantinovich. You've got it entirely wrong.

VIKTOR: Ya? Byezhat'? Zachem?

NADIA: Me? Defect? Why should I do that?

VIKTOR: U myenya v Moskvye pryekrasnaya kvartira, dacha v Zhukovkye...

NADIA: I have a beautiful apartment in Moscow, a dacha in Zhukovka...

VIKTOR: Ya byvayu za granitsei nyeskol'ko raz v godu...

NADIA: I make several foreign trips a year...

VIKTOR: U myenya nyet prichin pokidat' rodinu...

NADIA: Why should I want to defect?

VIKTOR: Poslushaitye...

NADIA: Listen...

VIKTOR: Eto vsyo dovol'no slozhno, prikhoditsya govorit' pri nyei...

NADIA: This is difficult for me, because I have to say things in front of this girl —

VIKTOR: [*hesitates*] No ya dolzhen skazat' eto, chtoby vy i Mister Pointer znali istinu.

NADIA: But I have to say them because you and Mr. Pointer have to understand.

VIKTOR: Moya kar'yera pod ugrozoi...

NADIA: My career is at stake.

VIKTOR: Moyo zhizn' pod ugrozoi...

NADIA: My life is at stake.

VIKTOR: Moyo dobroye imya pod somnyeniyem.

NADIA: My integrity is in doubt.

VIKTOR: Zhigalin mozhet podtvyerdit' kazhdoye moyo slovo, kogda protryezvyeyet.

NADIA: Zhigalin will support every word I say. When he sobers up.

VIKTOR: On godami yezdit so mnoi. On znayet myenya.

NADIA: He's been looking after me for years now. He knows me.

VIKTOR: Pravda, absolyutnaya pravda...

NADIA: The truth is, the absolute truth is...

VIKTOR: Vot ona vam: ya khotyel pyeryespat' s Miss Ogilvie-Smith.

NADIA: ...that I only wanted to — to — [*hesitates*] to get Miss Ogilvie-Smith into bed... to — to screw Miss Ogilvie-Smith.

VIKTOR: That's disgraceful, that's not what I said, you're
          deliberately misinterpreting me.
                    [GORKIN *grabs* VIKTOR *brutally by the hair and*
                    turns his face away from NADIA.]

GORKIN: Ty chto, nye ponyal?... Po-ikhnyemu ni slova!...

NADIA: [*translating*] No English, you understand me! No
          more English!

VIKTOR: Dyesyat' lyet nazad u nas vozniklo nyebol'shoye
          uvlyecheniye, nyebol'shoi roman v Nyu-Yorkye.

NADIA: Ten years ago, we had a little romance — an affair
          — a little affair in New York.

VIKTOR: Kogda ya uvidyelsya s nyei opyat' v etoi poyezd-
          kye...

NADIA: When I saw her again on this trip...

VIKTOR: Ya podumal: bylo by milo vozobnovit' otno-
          sheniya...

NADIA: I thought what fun it would be to have another little
          — [*slight hesitation*] — affair.

VIKTOR: Sami vyed' znayetye, trudnosti podstyogivayut mye-
          nya, ya lyublyu bor'bu.

NADIA: You know me, I like the pursuit, the chase, the chat.

VIKTOR: Soznayus', ya skazal yei, chto khochu ostat'sya.

NADIA: I admit I told her I wanted to defect.

VIKTOR: No znayetye zhenshchin...

NADIA: But you know what women are...

VIKTOR: Ikh nado kak-to zazhech i...

NADIA: Some you have to tell you lust after their bodies,
          others that you are fascinated by their intellect —
                    [VIKTOR *shakes his head despairingly at her trans-*
                    lation.]

VIKTOR: Nadya nye priznayot vryemyennykh romanov, ona
          vosprinimayet vsyo syer'yozno i po-etomu ya... nu
          ... znachit... ponimayetye

NADIA: In her case she wants stability, a future. All I
          wanted was to bed her. I tried lust, I tried love. In
          the end I told her what she wanted to hear —

VIKTOR: You are distorting my words, how can you do this to
          me? — [*to* POINTER] It is an entirely wrong inter-
          pretation.

GORKIN: Byelyayev, ni slova po-angliiski.

[GORKIN *grabs* VIKTOR *by the face and holds him so that he cannot look at her.*]

NADIA: Don't speak in English!

VIKTOR: Ya skazal, chto u nas yest' vozmozhnost' byt' vmyestye do kontsa nashikh dnyei.

NADIA: I put into her mind the possibility of sharing the rest of my life with her.

VIKTOR: Mozhetye nazvat' eto mirnym sosushchestvovaniyem...

NADIA: You could call it peaceful co-existence...

VIKTOR: ...razryadkoi.

NADIA: ...*détente.*

[GORKIN *smiles almost for the first time.*]

VIKTOR: Itak ya yei skazal, chto gotov byezhat'.

NADIA: And so, I told her I'd defect.

VIKTOR: Nye dumaitye, chtoby ya osobyenno gordilsya etim.

NADIA: I'm not saying it's admirable.

VIKTOR: No ya takov.

NADIA: But it's me.

VIKTOR: Vot kakoi ya muzhik.

NADIA: It's how I am.

VIKTOR: Dorozhu pobyedoi.

NADIA: I like the conquest.

VIKTOR: I, kak govorit ona, ya byesposhchadyen.

NADIA: And, as she says, I'm ruthless. [*correcting him*] No, cruel, vicious.

VIKTOR: Sprositye Zhigalina. Dogovorilis' s nim na etot shchyot.

NADIA: Ask Zhigalin. We have an arrangement.

VIKTOR: On nichevo nye vidit.

NADIA: He turns a blind eye.

VIKTOR: Raz u myenya zhenshchina, on uzhe vyshel za pokupkami.

NADIA: When I have a woman, he goes shopping.

[GORKIN *turns to* NADIA.]

GORKIN: [*hissing*] Ty — samka!

[NADIA *bows her head.*]

POINTER: What did he say?

NADIA: He called me a whore.

VIKTOR: He did not, he said you were a dangerous woman, nothing more —

GORKIN: [*exploding, to* POINTER] Chto eto vy, Pointer, tut stryapayetye? Khotitye s yeyo pomoshch'yu sprovotsirovat' intsidyent? [*to* VIKTOR] A ty vyegyosh' syebya kak naivnoye ditya. Pochemu imyenno ona? Chem privorozhila? Chto — u nyeyo po drugomu, chto li?

VIKTOR: Nye v tom dyelo. Tam prosto vsyo kak po maslu... vsyo kak po maslu...

[NADIA *begins to tremble.*]

POINTER: I'm sorry, Nadia, but I must know what's being said.

NADIA: Mr. Gorkin accuses you of using whores to create a diplomatic incident. He then remonstrated with Mr. Belaev for being — naive. Why her? Mr. Gorkin asked. There are so many fish in the sea. She seems rather unattractive to me. Perhaps she's good in bed. Mr. Belaev answered, very good, very adventurous. Total surrender.

VIKTOR: Eto vsyo nye tak!

NADIA: Podlyets!

VIKTOR: Sama vyed' znayesh', chto nye tak!

NADIA: Myerzavyets!

VIKTOR: Ya govoril sovsyem drugoye!....

NADIA: Trus!

[VIKTOR *talks to* GORKIN.]

VIKTOR: Nikolai Lyeonidovich vsyo obo mnye zhayet.

NADIA: Stepanov knows all about me.

VIKTOR: On dazhe nazyvayet myenya tovarishch Don Zhuan. Moya zhena tozhe vsyo znayet.

NADIA: As a matter of fact he calls me Comrade Don Juan. My wife also knows all about me.

VIKTOR: Ona nye protiv.

NADIA: She doesn't mind — you said you were divorced.

VIKTOR: Ya lyublyu svoyu zhenu, i ona myenya lyubit.

NADIA: I love my wife. And she loves me.

VIKTOR: Ona znayet kakov ya.

NADIA: She also knows what I'm like — she can't, she can't know.

VIKTOR: Yeyo eto nye volnuyet.

NADIA: It doesn't bother her — you bastard, you criminal bastard.

VIKTOR: My chudno zhivyom.

NADIA: We have a terrific life together — this man doesn't know lies from truth.

VIKTOR: Bud' u nyeyo lyubovnik, ya b yeyo ubil.

NADIA: But I'd kill her if I found out she had a lover — why not kill the lover?

VIKTOR: Klyanus' vam, Lyev Konstantinovich, vot i vsya istoriya.

NADIA: I swear to you, Lev Konstantinovich, that's all there is to it.

VIKTOR: Eto tol'ko byezzlobnaya shutka...

NADIA: It was a little harmless fun — not harmless, no.

VIKTOR: [to NADIA] ...poiski naslazhdyeniya.

NADIA: ...the pursuit of happiness.

VIKTOR: Vsye muzhiki takiye.

NADIA: We're all men of the world.

VIKTOR: Sami zhe ponimayetye...

NADIA: We're all men of the world. You understand.

> [NADIA *cries out in pain.*
>
> POINTER *covers his face with a hand.*
>
> GORKIN *laughs and pats* VIKTOR *on the back.* VIK-TOR *smiles crookedly.*
>
> *Slow fade to blackout.*]

Lights on GORKIN *and* VIKTOR.

GORKIN *wears headphones, listening to a simultaneous translation. He makes notes.*

VIKTOR *addresses the inquiry.*

VIKTOR: Mr. Gorkin and I would like to thank you for allowing us to present an objective point of view. With the greatest courtesy, I must ask you to put aside any pre-conceptions you may have in relation to a Soviet diplomat. We are all conditioned to think of each other in a particular light, and not always a favourable light. I ask you to regard me simply as a human being in crisis. Let me say at the outset that not everything was accurately interpreted after the party. I tried to intervene but circumstances rendered my attempts ineffective. For example, Miss Ogilvie-Smith interpreted general remarks made by Mr. Gorkin as personal insults. He never called her a whore. If you ask why she should put such words into his mouth, I can only give my own value judgement: she was accusing herself, out of shame and guilt. But the heart of the matter is this: would I, in my position, say I was going to defect simply in order to seduce a woman? Would any man? Forgive me for saying so, but I believe this to be a laughable proposition. In all modesty, I have no need to resort to such a ruse. [*He smiles, remembering his joke.*] If you ask me to analyse Miss Ogilvie Smith's behaviour, I am bound to say she is a romantic. A fantasist. The idea that I was going to defect was born of her fantasy, not mine. My mistake was to encourage her. I never thought for a moment she would take me seriously. She wants nothing that is painful or unpleasant yet she cannot take human relationships lightly. This is bound to cause suffering. And furthermore, Mr. Gorkin has asked me to say —

> [*Surreptitiously,* VIKTOR *unplugs* GORKIN's *headphones. While* GORKIN *fiddles to get back the sound,* VIKTOR *speaks quickly without changing his physical position.*]

Mr. Pointer, please give her a message from me. Tell her I am not criminal but human. Tell her I am not cruel but cowardly. Tell her I am not vicious but concupiscent. And tell her I am crushed by remorse.

> [*He replugs the headphones and continues in the same voice as before.*]

— every sympathy for her. I take comfort in the thought that I gave her many pleasures in the few days we were together.

[GORKIN *taps* VIKTOR *on the arm and hands him
the copy of 'Heartbreak House'.*]

Yes. Mr. Gorkin has reminded me that we must
return her copy of the play. He says he would not
like her to think of us as thieves.

[GORKIN *smiles, nods appreciatively and hands* VIK-
TOR *a note.*]

Mr. Gorkin also thanks you for handling the matter
in such a discreet way. He hopes, in turn, you
appreciate our co-operation. He would be very unhappy if this affair was to be leaked, or in any way
allowed to disturb the forthcoming visit of President
Stepanov. It is a question of priorities.

[*Pause.*]

May I add something on my own behalf? Whatever
you decide about Miss Ogilvie-Smith's future, I ask
you, as gentlemen, not to be too hard on her.

[*Lights fade.*]

Lights on the living room.

SOPHIA *is playing cards.* POINTER, *briefcase in hand, has
just arrived.*

POINTER: I've come to see Nadia. Where is she?

SOPHIA: Working.

POINTER: Working? I thought she was too ill —

SOPHIA: She works, she sleeps, she weeps, she wakes. It is not
at this moment a good life.

POINTER: What is she working on?

SOPHIA: Dostoevsky, Chekhov, I don't know. Translation.
She is interpreter with Foreign Office. Vocabulary
amazing, accent awful.

[NADIA *enters. She wears a dressing-gown. She
walks with difficulty. Her left hand trembles.*]

NADIA: I thought I heard voices.

SOPHIA: Ah, so you are here.

POINTER: .[*sickeningly sympathetic*] Nadia, how are you?

NADIA: Sitting up and taking nourishment, thank you.

[*Awkward pause.*]

Baboushka, Mr. Pointer has come to see me on a

private matter. Would you like to go to your bed-room now?

SOPHIA: No.

POINTER: [*to* NADIA] It's all right. If you don't mind, I don't.

NADIA: What's the decision?

POINTER: The inquiry has come to the conclusion that it would be best if you resigned.

NADIA: What reasons will I give?

POINTER: Ill health.

> [*He takes a letter from his briefcase.*]

NADIA: Good, so long as it isn't the truth.

POINTER: I really think this is the best way out.

> [*He lays the letter before her. She reads it. She stares into space.*]

NADIA: It's quite true. I'm not well. If I cry suddenly please don't be embarrassed, I — [*She holds out her hand.*] — I can't control my hand either. They give me seda-tives. But they're not strong enough.

POINTER: I just wanted to bring you the news in person. I didn't want you further upset by a cold, official communication.

NADIA: Thank you.

> [*She picks the letter up. It flaps alarmingly.* POIN-TER *gently takes it from her hand, lays it on the desk and holds out a pen for her. She tries to steady herself.*]

POINTER: I do wish you'd talked to me, Nadia. I could perhaps have helped.

NADIA: I was in love with him, how could you have helped? I realise it's not a rational explanation, as a matter of fact it's rather banal, nevertheless the pain won't go away just because it's trivial. You don't die from toothache either, but — [*She loses concentration.*] I've been put through it. Through the minefield, that is. Oblivion seems the only answer, but I wouldn't give anyone the satisfaction of that, certainly not Viktor Belaev, not even me —

SOPHIA: Belaev, Belaev? Why you speak of this man? He is anti-Christ.

NADIA: [*vehemently*] I don't care if he's anti-Christ. Christ can take care of himself. I care that he's anti-human, anti-me.

SOPHIA: Me, me, me.

NADIA: The truth, if you want to know, the truth is I was a willing victim, I connived, I wanted to believe the lies. [*referring to* SOPHIA] I can't talk to her, she doesn't understand what's going on, nor do I, she lives faithful to her own past, not to mine, it's not her fault, but I have no one to talk to. I was lonely. Any person without someone to love is lonely. I love him. He talked to me but he lied. He couldn't tell lies from truth. Can you? My dear Viktor not only lied to me, he also lied to himself. The result is he's lost all respect for the truth, for himself, for others, for me. Some things are very clear. If you can't respect, there's no love, and if you can't love the void is filled with worms and maggots. And, would you believe it, it all comes from lying to yourself.

[*She breaks off and sits frozen, staring.*]

[*snapping back*] One can never learn from other people's experience, isn't that odd? It seems we all have to go through the minefield ourselves to believe it exists. There was a girl, Olya Rashidova was her name. She warned me. She'd stepped on a mine. She said my dear Vitya was out to conquer a woman of every nationality in the United Nations. [*She laughs.*] He must have done rather well. They didn't recall him until he screwed the United Kingdom. [*She begins to lose concentration.*] Lucky Yemen. Lucky Zimbabwe —

[*She is lost again.*]

POINTER: Sign the letter now, Nadia, and I'll go.

NADIA: [*snapping back*] My heart is broken. The house has fallen down.

POINTER: Oh yes. [*He reaches into his briefcase.*] They asked me to return this.

[*He hands over a copy of the play.*]

NADIA: Nothing else? No personal message? Nothing?

POINTER: [*implacable*] No. No personal message. Nothing.

NADIA: I sometimes think he was right: I was born to suffer.

POINTER: That's absolute nonsense, I can't bear all that self-indulgence. [*Pause.*] I'm sorry. [*Pause.*] I'm not good at this sort of thing. I think it's well-known I'm rather a dry old stick. I'm from the North. We don't flaunt our feelings. That doesn't mean I don't have sympathy for you. I do. I sympathise deeply. I was ashamed of myself the other night, here, in this room, allowing you to interpret what I can only describe as that obscene confession. Of course, we believe *your* version of events. At least, I do. And I want to help you. We all want to help you. As a matter of fact, the Secretary of State asked me to say how sorry he was. But resignation is the best way out. For us, of course, it is, I admit that freely, but also for you. And we'll help. We'll all rally round. There'll be language courses for you to teach, translations —

SOPHIA: Nadia, why do you cry? More tears than snowflakes in *Casse Noisette*. Why, why? Why cry for that skunk? [*to* POINTER] And you, you are not much better. I am old woman, listen to me. I know nothing, but this I know. You sit side by side with them, mutual interest, you give me nausea. Business cannot be done with these people. But, this falls on deaf ears. I am old, yes, of the past, yes. Maybe new attitude is required. I say not. Skunk does not change smell. You are intelligentsia. You know what intelligentsia respect most in the whole world? Not God, not people, not human feelings, no. Intelligentsia respect only one thing: power. Disgusting.

POINTER: Sign the letter, Nadia. Go away. Rest. Get strong. Then, we can talk again. We'll find something for you to do.

NADIA: I know what I want to do. I don't want to give in. I'm not going to give in. I presume the pain will ease. Sooner or later. Probably later. And then I will be something more than I am now. I'll look back on this and may even be able to smile, as the Russians say. If I interpret them correctly. I shall try to conduct my life decently. That's all I can do. That's all any of us can do. [*She cries.*] I was gullible, I wanted to believe — look at my hand, just look at it — I must hold on. I must find faith in something. In taking the next breath, if nothing else. At least we should pretend to know why we live. We should believe in something that gets us through from day to day. Otherwise, nothing matters, nothing in the world. We simply have to go on. Of course, I don't believe in any of that nonsense about peace and happiness reigning, and of angels, and seeing the heavens covered in stars like diamonds. I don't believe that. I don't believe in heaven or earth. I just believe in holding on as decently —

> [*Silence.*]

SOPHIA: Eto chelovek ushol? On skazal do svidaniya?

NADIA: She asked if the man has gone, if he said goodbye. Which man, Baboushka?

SOPHIA: Mnye prisnilos'.

NADIA: She says she was dreaming.

SOPHIA: Get dressed, Nadia. Make yourself pretty.

NADIA: I wish I didn't love him so much.

SOPHIA: The cards are full of promise.

> [*She sleeps.*]

NADIA: I want to believe in anything that makes this pain seem worthwhile. [*She looks at* POINTER.] You're crying. Well, that's something, I suppose —

> [*She signs the letter.*
>
> *Lights fade.*
>
> *Blackout.*]

THE END

Other books by Ronald Harwood

Novels:
All the Same Shadows
The Guilt Merchants
The Girl in Melanie Klein
Articles of Faith
The Genoa Ferry
Cesar and Augusta

Short Stories:
One. Interior. Day. *Adventures in the Film Trade*

Biography:
Sir Donald Wolfit CBE: *His life and work in the unfashionable theatre**

Plays:
A Family
The Ordeal of Gilbert Pinfold (from Evelyn Waugh)*
The Dresser*
After the Lions*
Tramway Road*
The Deliberate Death of a Polish Priest*

Miscellaneous:
A Night at the Theatre (Editor)
The Ages of Gielgud (Editor)
All the World's a Stage

* *Published by Amber Lane Press*